D1524837

SAYVILLE LIBRARY

LEAD

A TRUE BOOK®

by
Salvatore Tocci

Children's Press®
A Division of Scholastic Inc.

New York Toronto London Auckland Sydney
Mexico City New Delhi Hong Kong
Danbury, Connecticut

Lead bricks made from old car batteries are stacked at a recycling center in France.

Reading Consultant
Julia McKenzie Munemo, MEd
New York, New York

Science Consultant
John A. Benner
Austin, Texas

The photo on the cover shows lead ore. The photo on the title page shows lead pellets.

The author and the publisher are not responsible for injuries or accidents that occur during or from any experiments. Experiments should be conducted in the presence of or with the help of an adult. Any instructions of the experiments that require the use of sharp, hot, or other unsafe items should be conducted by or with the help of an adult.

Library of Congress Cataloging-in-Publication Data

Tocci, Salvatore.
  Lead / by Salvatore Tocci.
    p. cm. — (A true book)
  Includes bibliographical references and index.
  ISBN 0-516-23699-7 (lib. bdg.)   0-516-25575-4 (pbk.)
  1. Lead—Juvenile literature. I. Title. II. Series.
QD181.P3T63 2005
546'.688—dc22   2004027155

© 2005 by Salvatore Tocci.
All rights reserved. Published in 2005 by Children's Press, an imprint of Scholastic Library Publishing. Published simultaneously in Canada.
Printed in the United States of America.

CHILDREN'S PRESS, and A TRUE BOOK™, and associated logos are trademarks and/or registered trademarks of Scholastic Library Publishing.
SCHOLASTIC and associated logos are trademarks and/or registered trademarks of Scholastic Inc.
1 2 3 4 5 6 7 8 9 10 R 14 13 12 11 10 09 08 07 06 05

Contents

You can see through glass
because light can pass
through it.

What Can You See?

Name something you can see through. Chances are you said a window or glass. Glass is transparent, which means that light can pass through it. Some things are not transparent because they do not allow light to pass through them. As a result, you cannot see through them.

5

One thing you cannot see through is a person's body. For a long time, doctors wished that they had some way of seeing inside a sick person's body. They knew that if they could, they might be better able to help the person.

In 1895, a German scientist discovered a way to look inside a person's body. He discovered rays that could pass through heavy black paper. He called them X-rays.

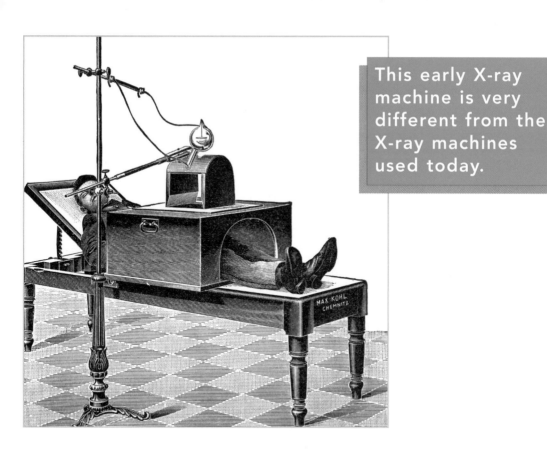

This early X-ray machine is very different from the X-ray machines used today.

The scientist also discovered that X-rays would pass through a person's body so that the bones could be seen. By 1896, X-rays were being used to identify bone fractures.

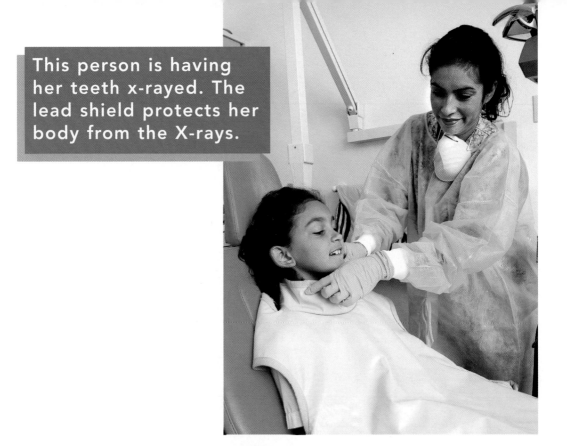

This person is having her teeth x-rayed. The lead shield protects her body from the X-rays.

About fifty years later, scientists began to realize that although X-rays were useful, they were also dangerous. Exposing someone to too many X-rays could cause serious illness, such as cancer. As a result, they began to put a shield over the patient so that only the area they wanted to examine was exposed to the X-rays. The rest of the body was protected by the shield, which did not allow X-rays to pass through it. The shield contained a substance called lead. These lead shields are still used by X-ray technicians and other medical professionals today.

What Is Lead?

Lead is an **element**. An element is a building block of **matter**. Matter is the stuff or material that makes up everything in the universe. This book, the chair you are sitting on, and even your body are all made of matter.

There are millions of different kinds of matter. There are,

Lead is one of the elements that make up stained-glass windows.

however, just a few more than one hundred different elements. It is hard to believe that so many different **compounds** can be created with only one hundred or so different elements.

It may help you to understand this idea if you think about the English language. It contains just twenty-six letters, but they can be arranged to make up all the words in the language. Similarly, the one hundred or so elements can be put together in different ways to make up all the different kinds of matter in the universe.

Every element has both a name and a symbol that consists of one, two, or three letters. The symbol for lead is Pb, which comes from the Latin word for lead, *plumbum.*

The ancient Romans used lead to make pipes for plumbing. Can you tell where the word *plumbing* comes from? Some of these lead pipes are still used today. The Romans also used lead to line containers in which they stored food and water.

Lead was first used by people long before the ancient Romans used it. Lead objects have been found in Egyptian tombs that date back to 8,500 years ago.

Lead can sometimes be found as an element in nature. Lead is more commonly found in **ores**, however. An ore is an example of a compound, which

The layers of this lead ore show the growth of crystals over time.

is made when two or more different elements combine to form one substance. One of the more common lead ores is called galena. This ore is a compound made of lead and another element called sulfur.

Like most other elements, lead is a metal. The one property that all metals have in common is their ability to conduct electricity.

Most metals also share some other properties. For example,

Lead has a bluish-gray color.

Metals that are ductile can be made into wires like the ones that make up this barbed wire fence.

most metals are **malleable**, which means that they can be hammered or pressed into thin sheets. Most metals are also **ductile**, which means that they can be drawn out into a thin wire.

Lead is one of the softer metals, so it can be shaped more easily than many other metals. Although it is soft, lead is still a strong metal that does not crack easily from wear or age.

Lead is also quite heavy. In fact, it is heavier than about eighty of the other elements. Scientists find it useful to compare substances such as elements in terms of their **density** rather than their

This bar of ancient Roman lead weighs more than 66 pounds (30 kilograms).

weight. Density is a measure-
ment of how much matter is
present in a given volume or
space. For example, you
could say that the population
density of your room is twice
as great when there are four
people in it as when there are
two people in it. The density
of lead is greater than that of
most other elements. This
density is what makes lead
useful for protecting people
against X-rays.

Measuring Lead's Density

Density is calculated by dividing the mass of an object by its volume. Mass is a quantity recorded in units such as grams. Volume is a quantity recorded in units such as milliliters.

Obtain a lead sinker used for fishing. The mass may be recorded on the sinker in grams. If it is not, measure its mass using a scale that measures mass in grams.

Next, find a small measuring cup or a graduated cylinder that is marked in milliliters. Fill it to the 100-milliliter mark with water. Carefully drop the sinker into the water. Record the new water level in the measuring cup or graduated cylinder. The difference between 100 milliliters and the new water level is the volume of the lead sinker.

Scientists express density as grams per milliliter. To figure out the density of the lead sinker, divide its mass by its volume. The density of lead is about 11 grams per milliliter. How close was your value to the actual density of lead?

How Is Lead Useful?

Lead is used to make **solder.** Solder is made by mixing lead with tin, which is another metallic element. It is an example of an **alloy**, which is a substance that is made by mixing a metal with one or more other elements. Solder is used to join metal parts.

An important use of lead solder is in the making of circuit boards. They are used in electronic devices such as computers and cellular telephones.

When solder is used to join metal parts, it is heated to its melting point and then allowed to cool. Lead has a low melting point compared to most metals. This allows the heat to melt the solder but not the metal parts that are to be joined. As the solder turns back into a solid, it forms a strong bond between the metal parts.

Lead is used not only to make alloys but also to make compounds. Some of these lead compounds are used as pigments in paints. For example, compounds made of lead and oxygen are used as yellow and reddish-brown pigments. Another lead compound is used for making fireworks.

Nearly 80 percent of the lead used today is used for making car batteries. Car batteries use both

Car batteries are collected for recycling.

pure lead and a lead compound. These lead substances are sealed in a solution of acid. That is why a car battery is known as a lead-acid battery.

A car's battery provides enough energy to start the car's engine. Once the car is running, the battery is recharged. A lead-acid battery can go through many thousands of recharges before it finally fails to start the car.

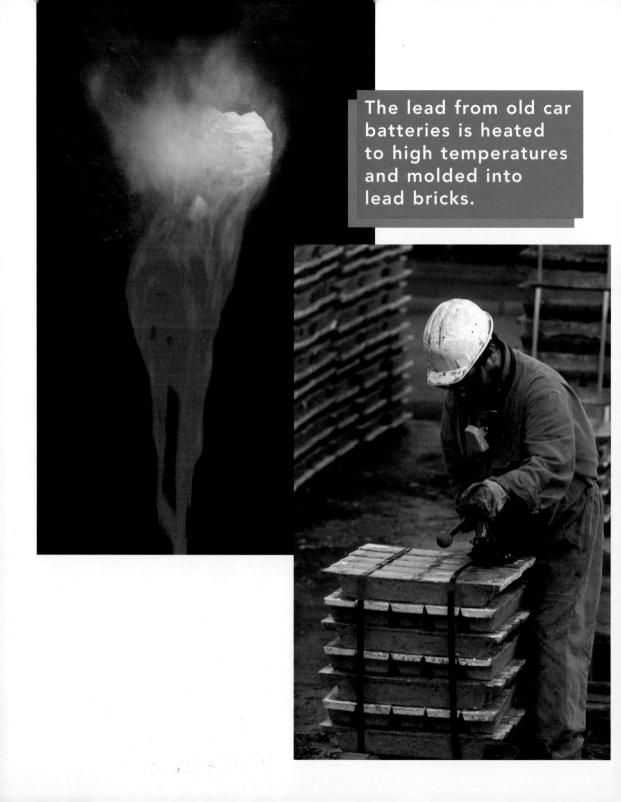

The lead from old car batteries is heated to high temperatures and molded into lead bricks.

"Dead" car batteries were once just thrown into the garbage. This was a dangerous practice. Today, they are recycled. This way, the lead can be reused so that it doesn't end up in the ground, where it could con- tribute to lead poisoning.

SAYVILLE LIBRARY

What Is Lead Poisoning?

Inside the body, lead is a poison. Symptoms of lead poisoning include a poor appetite, a stomachache, a tired feeling, a headache, and trouble sleeping. Higher levels of lead can damage the kidneys and brain. Over a period of time, having a

Lead poisoning poses the greatest risk to children under the age of six because their bodies are growing so rapidly.

high level of lead in the body can cause mental and behavioral problems.

Lead can get into a person's body from various sources. Lead was once added to paint to make it dry faster and last longer. About 75 percent of homes in the United States built before 1978 contain lead paint. The paint used in homes built before 1960 may contain an even higher amount of lead.

Paint that peels off of a wall in one of these older homes can be a problem. A young child may pick up a paint chip

Chipped and peeling paint doesn't just look bad. It can be a health hazard if the paint contains lead.

from the floor and eat it because the lead gives the paint chip a sweet taste.

Lead, however, is more likely to get into a person's body from paint dust. Over many years, some of the paint on walls, ceilings, and doors slowly crumbles into dust. This dust may fall on toys that children put into their mouths. As children crawl or play on the floor their hands may also pick up the dust. The lead in the dust then gets into their bodies when they put their hands in their mouths.

Testing for Lead

You can use a test kit sold in hardware stores or over the Internet to check for lead in paint, drinking water, or plumbing pipes. These kits contain swabs that can be wiped on any surface. If lead is present, a distinct color appears on the swab. If lead is present in your home, you should check the online sources listed in this book to find out what your family should do.

Lead test kit

Dust that contains lead may also come from outdoors. Lead was once added to gasoline to improve the performance of car engines. This lead was released into the air in the waste gases and vapors from the car. Lead is also released into the air by incinerators, furnaces that are used for burning waste materials. Lead is found in the soil, too. This lead comes mainly from the outsides of buildings that have

In 1996, the U.S. government banned the use of lead in gasoline.

been covered with lead paint. Lead in the soil may find its way into homes as dust.

Once the dangers of lead poisoning were recognized,

laws were passed to ban its use. In 1977, the U.S. government banned the sale of any paint that contained lead. The use of food cans sealed with lead solder was also banned. At one time, lead pipes were used for plumbing. Today, lead pipes can no longer be used for plumbing that is used to carry drinking water. Since these bans were passed, the levels of lead in water, land, air, and homes has greatly decreased.

Lead pipes can no longer be used in plumbing.

Lead, like many other elements, must be handled properly. As careful consumers, we need to be aware of lead's usefulness as well as its dangers. Then we can choose to use lead in ways that do not harm our environment.

Fun Facts About Lead

- A pencil does not contain any lead. Pencil "lead" is actually graphite, which is made from the element carbon.

- The National Wildlife Federation encourages the use of nonlead sinkers for fishing to help prevent lead poisoning in waterfowl.

- Each year, about 20 million pounds (9 million kilograms) of lead solder are used worldwide.

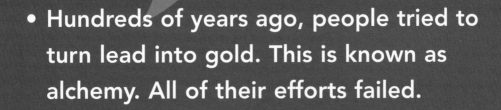

- Hundreds of years ago, people tried to turn lead into gold. This is known as alchemy. All of their efforts failed.

- Lead has been found in distant stars in the Milky Way galaxy. The lead in each star weighs about the same as our moon.

- The oldest known lead object is a statue that was found in Turkey and is more than eight thousand years old.

To Find Out More

To find out more about lead, check out these additional sources.

Books

Baldwin, Carol. **Metals.** Raintree Steck-Vaughn, 2004.

Oxlade, Chris. **Elements and Compounds.** Heinemann Library, 2002.

Tocci, Salvatore. **The Periodic Table.** Children's Press, 2004.

Watt, Susan. **Lead.** Benchmark Books, 2001.

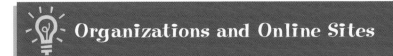

Organizations and Online Sites

About Lead

*http://enviro.nfesc.navy.mil/
esc425/AbtLead.htm*

Visit this site for more information about the history of lead and to learn why lead is useful in many different products.

**It's Elemental–
The Element Lead**

*http://education.jlab.org/its
elemental/ele082.html*

Log on to learn more about lead and the alloys and compounds it forms.

Lead Poisoning

*http://www.niehs.nih.gov/
kids/lead.htm*

Learn more about the sources of lead poisoning and what you can do if this danger exists in your home.

**Lead Poisoning:
From Beethoven to Ducks**

*http://www.riverdeep.net/
current/2000/11/110800_l
ead.jhtml*

Did the famous composer Ludwig van Beethoven die from lead poisoning? Why are ducks facing the threat of lead poisoning? You can find the answers to these questions along with other interesting facts about lead on this site.

Important Words

alloy substance made by mixing a metal with one or more other elements

compound substance formed when two or more elements are combined

density amount of matter in a given volume

ductile capable of being drawn into a wire

element building block of matter

malleable capable of being hammered into a layer or thin sheet

matter stuff or material that makes up everything in the universe

ore material found in nature from which a valuable substance, such as lead, can be extracted

solder alloy that contains lead and is used to join metal parts

Index

Meet the Author

Salvatore Tocci is a science writer who lives in East Hampton, New York, with his wife, Patti. He was a high school biology and chemistry teacher for almost thirty years. His books include a high school chemistry textbook and an elementary school book series that encourages students to perform experiments to learn about science. In his free time, Mr. Tocci enjoys sailing. The keel on his sailboat contains 5,000 pounds (2,265 kg) of lead for ballast.

Photographs © 2005: Corbis Images: 7 (Bettman), 41 (Jim Craigmyle); Corbis Sygma/Alain Nogues: 2, 28, 30; Fundamental Photos, New York/Michael Dalton: 35; James Levin/Studio 10: 37; Photo Researchers, NY: 20 (Volker Steger), 15 (Dirk Wiersma); PhotoEdit: 4 (Bill Aron), 25 (Spencer Grant), 11 (Jeff Greenberg), 8, 33, 39 (Michael Newman), 18 (Jonathan A. Nourok); Visuals Unlimited: 17 (Inga Spence), 1 (Larry Stepanowicz), cover (William J. Weber).

SAYVILLE LIBRARY
11 COLLINS AVE.
SAYVILLE, NY 11782

SEP 2 6 2005